The

Sundress Publications • Knoxville, TN

ISBN: 978-1-939675-68-2
Library of Congress: 2018931079
Published by Sundress Publications
www.sundresspublications.com

Editor: Erin Elizabeth Smith
Editorial Assistant: Macy French

Special thanks to Danielle Hayden and Cassie M. Grillon.

Colophon: This book is set in Adobe Garamond Pro.

Cover Image by Dzika Mrowka.

Cover Design: Kristen Ton

Book Design: Erin Elizabeth Smith

The Minor Territories
Danielle Sellers

Thanks

I would like to thank Carrie Fountain, without whose astute guidance many of these poems would not have been. Thank you to Erin Elizabeth Smith and Sundress Publications, as well as Christine Davis, Corinna McClanahan Schroeder, Andrea Luttrell, Greg Brownderville, Traci Brimhall, Beth Ann Fennelly, Gary Short, Ann Fisher-Wirth, Debora Greger, Bill Logan, Anna Leahy, Chloe Honum, Heather Matesich Cousins, Heather Price, Claire Mischker, J. Gabriel Scala, Alicia Casey, and Chris Hayes. Thanks to you, AS. Thanks also to Gemini Ink Mentorship Program, the Workshops at Djerassi Resident Artists Program, The Sewanee Writers' Conference, The University of Mississippi, as well as John and Renee Grisham for their financial support. To my Mama and my girl Olivia: y'all are everything.

Contents

Part III

For Olivia, who makes it all worth it.

"To honor the present
and honor the past, be in the present

and not shut off the past– "

–Ann Fisher-Wirth, *Carta Marina*

Late October, Sardis Lake

We were not yet married. Our bean-
child swung, suspended in my belly, shrimp-clear.
That time of year, the camp fires were few,
just dots of light along the lake edge.
At the next camp, a man beat hell
out of his boy. Owl feathers drifted to the fire.
My fiancé hoped ours would not be a son.

The sun lost to a dark moon.
We argued over the proper way
to begin a long night's blaze.
When the vein in his temple throbbed,
I sputtered and turned in. He eyed the ax,
raised the volume on the radio.
Against the night, our neighbors' flames
looked like couples kissing. I thought,
There are ways to lose a thing so small.

I.

She chooses the known wild, tired now...
—Claudia Emerson, "Westerns"

A Waiting Room in Kuwait

On the terrazzo floor, a sea
of soldiers in desert fatigues,
use their packs as pillows,
wait for a flight home
or back to war. All of them
want to be anywhere but there.

At a bank of outdated computers
in a metal folding chair,
my old high school boyfriend finds me
on the Internet. I was a poetry student
with promise, just beginning to publish.

He'd often thought of me, he said.
I hadn't thought of him in years.
But the stacks were lonely,
and he was a safe distance.
What harm could there be
in giving him a home to call?

I'd seen the news. So many
dying every day,
every day. When he called,
his voice was low, gentle,
and broken by static.

A Photo of the Euphrates

I wasn't expecting that green on the bank,
paper-money palm trees or potato vines.
A thin woman in river-soaked rags waves,
a net bursting with muddy clothes.
Despite the Army's presence, she grins,
toothless, happy with her work.

He remembers the red tights I wore
beneath my cheerleader skirt,
the scent of river on skin,
and bikini bottoms drifting
from my body that anchored his.
He loved me enough to find me again.

Since then, his tongue has changed
the river's story. He's killed strangers
on its shore. I imagine him lying
on the dusty floor of a marble palace
at sundown, breathing red air,
waiting for the comfort night gives.

He's ready for what may happen.
I worry he won't make it back
untouched. For now, I'm happy
to let him imagine me still a girl
with a ponytail and red lips on Friday nights,
kicking the moon in its eye.

Beautiful Dreamers

Before dawn's last detonation,
   the soldiers talk of war movies,
the terse and inaccurate dialogue,
   absurd tactics and kill shots.

They talk of the river instead of home.
   It's best to patrol under date palms,
where a breeze lifts the sun-rags
   knotted at the napes of their necks.

They like least to trek the ridges
   in daylight, where heat can be seen,
its waves and smoky arrows, floaters against
   the cornea. Tonight, they want

more than anything to turn in,
   to feel against their groins
the blossoms of cool sheets,
   to dream of home and never wake.

Letter From the Velvet Ditch 1
Oxford, Mississippi

While he patrols the dark streets
banked by sewage, I learn
the art of baking French bread. I have nothing
but time. In my warm kitchen,
yeast fills the lung of its loaf and sighs.
I bake and bake and bake.

I imagine him in Iraq, dusty, blistered,
knees and elbows rock-scraped, but mostly
unharmed. I do not think about those
trying to shoot him or who he's shot.

From Mississippi, I send letters
he says he keeps under his helmet,
the words of my cursive
script close to his shaved scalp.
Sweat softens the perfumed paper.
The ink runs.

Instead of IEDs, I imagine the market
strong with anise and cardamom,
goat hocks, thin calves' slit throats.
Baskets of rice bleaching in the sun.
He scoops a handful, lets it sift
through his fingers like sand.

I count down his return to Germany,
have a ticket to meet him there.
He has promised beers in tall glasses,
cheese fondue, a diamond ring.

I make a list of things to do:
can the wild figs, choose the holiday turkey,
divide and separate the daylilies,
quilt the summer-wounded beds with pine
before fall's frost invades,
before the maples surrender their shields.

L'empire de la Mort

After my grandmother died,
my mother and I treated ourselves

to Paris on her dime. We didn't want anyone
to say that we had never lived. That first night,

my belly full of good wine and cheese,
I came home to news of an ambush in Al Anbar.

My boyfriend had been shot and was,
at that moment, in surgery. Condition unknown.

All those casualty reports, the contents
of his kill letter, the life we'd been planning

in his down time, all seemed dim and far off.
Worry clouded the trip. In the Louvre,

I thought of that clunky piano ballad
I learned to play when I was just a girl,

my chubby fingers tripping over one another:
Que sera sera, whatever will be will be.

My mother thought it would be a good idea
to tour the catacombs.

The walls of femurs punctuated with skulls
rose overhead like muddy frozen waves.

We exhausted ourselves walking
and still there were thousands of years'

worth of bones. I remember thinking,
these were once people

who carried baskets through markets,
who loved and fucked and had stuffed noses,

who knew what it was like
to have dirt under their fingernails,

who drank wine and cured meats,
warmed their cold feet by fire.

Now just anonymous brown bones
reduced to minerals in an abandoned quarry.

It was then I decided:
If he lived through the war, I'd marry him.

The Germany Poems

I.

It was bright and clear when I arrived
in Frankfurt. February had been
a blur of grey. In the taxi
to the American base town, he said
I'd brought the sun. A fast polka
on the radio. An accordion's huff and whine
serenaded our first kiss in eleven years.

At the hotel, we barely got
the key through the door
before my clothes were off and I was under
his broad chest in my white lace bra.
He couldn't believe I was there.
He was dreaming. He was burning
inside me. That night

at the brau haus, I went without panties
in a short dress. The steaks came
buttered on a hot plate,
and I wanted to straddle him
at the table. On the long walk home,
he took me against someone's wall,
rough and fast, the way we both needed.

II.

That church bell, the waiting,
the purr of pigeons,
that papery castle on the hill,
nearly crumbling

with each cold gust of wind.

III.

Among the lichened ruins
of Heidelberg castle,
I reached for him
and for the first time he pulled away.

That night, I rented
a room in the best hotel.
We ate filet mignon with capers.
It nearly snowed at the table.

When he turned in
I cracked open his email account,
read his letters
to that Dallas blonde.

He told her
he was here
touring the *Altstadt*
with his Army pals.

IV.

For a summer, I lived in a small room I rented from a mountainous
German named Rolf. The room had two single beds, a digital alarm clock,
a snowy television, a rectangular bureau, a nightstand, a lamp, and a
bathroom with a shower. When he was off duty, we'd push together the
beds, watch German talk shows where men dressed like women and
women dressed like milkmaids. I was dying to see more of Europe. The
sliding glass door opened onto a poured concrete balcony which
overlooked the *Bahnhopf* and a roof. On the roof lived two standard

schnauzers. Their fur was matted. They drank from puddles and slept in barrels turned on their sides. Every morning Rolf set out breakfast: coffee, tea, boiled eggs, sausage, isosceles triangles of *Käse*, yogurt with honey, dried apples, warm *Brötchen*, butter, orange marmalade. It was pleasant to sit in the wood-paneled dining room and read. Back then I was reading *The Travels of Marco Polo*. I asked him once about the dogs on the roof. *Oh ja!,* he said. His face crinkled. *Those are mine. Aren't they fine?*

V.

Those nights he couldn't leave the base,
I came to him. His Army brothers hadn't seen
an American girl in months. They knew
all about me, even though he was the silent type.
Young German prostitutes roamed the halls
in spandex skirts. It was rumored the base
was closing. There was a sense of urgency
in their eyes. In the MEN ONLY bathroom,
condoms undulated in the toilets like sea anemones.
His roommate was blond and had a buzz
cut. He was lithe and dimpled,
spoke in a country accent, the kind of guy
I went for in my early twenties.
They had built a wall between their cots
with Budweiser cans. Our dates
were action movies and video games
that simulated flying. And when we tired
of that there was burgers and bowling.
Yet all I wanted to do was sit quietly
across from one another. I wanted him
to see me. Really see me.

VI.

That library of yellow books
in a language he couldn't read.
That *Bahnhopf* across the street,
those trains and the absence of trains.

VII.

His barracks,
the thinly partitioned
rooms, the velvet
mini-skirts
of German teenagers
trying for babies.

IX.

I wanted a baby. Other men
in the future
were like dim figures.
I could barely make out
their features. And here he was
with eyes so blue they lit the room.

X.

That Friedberg *Gasthaus.*
That dark-paneled dining room,
that breakfast of bitter coffee cold meat warm rolls.
That upstairs room with two singles struggled together.
That balcony overlooking the schnauzers
who lived on the roof, who drank from puddles.
I wanted to rescue them, all of them—

Bad Nauheim Train Station: After War
a zuihitsu

We waited for the ICE train to Frankfurt on metal benches.
My hand on the curve of his bicep, his hand in his coat pocket.
A cold clear morning, and our breath-smoke funnels the air.

***

Bad Nauheim is a spa town in the Rhineland. Its salt springs are used to
treat heart and nerve diseases.

***

On our walk through the Kurpark, the brown gurgle of a thermal fountain
sent him back to war. *Just a sad memory*, he said. I knew not to ask what.

***

Newspaper magnate William Randolph Hearst came to Bad Nauheim each
year with his mistress. In 1931, he met Mussolini here; and from here flew
to Berlin to meet Hitler in 1934.

***

In the garden beds, tulips raised their green temples. I thought of the
photograph he sent me while he was in Iraq: a man's face split open, his
skin like plum skin folded over his black hair. A hand on the pebble-and-
casing-strewn street, a fly on that hand. When I asked him why he sent me
that, he said he didn't know. He never did it again.

***

At night, I fingered the bullets like marbles under the skin of his shoulder.

***

Hearst did "much good" in advising Hitler to stop his persecution of the Jews. Afterward he spent his life trying to erase the name: *supporter of the Nazi cause.*

***

While deployed, he looked me up on the internet, sent an email with a picture of him and his daughter on a fishing boat.

***

After his divorce, we dated long distance for eight months. I sent care packages filled with lollipops for the Iraqi children in his village. He sent back sweat-creased notes. He had two kill letters: one addressed to me, the other to his daughter, to be delivered *in case.* I was dying to know what was in mine.

***

Here in Germany, he couldn't help but scan the rooftops for snipers, found himself walking backwards: *pulling rear detail.* I thought, *He'll be fine. He just needs time.*

***

Sex after a year at war was not as good as one might think.

***

In Cologne, I bought a black and white postcard taken after World War II. In it, the bridge to the train station is severed, its metal arcs twisted and breaking the flow of the Rhine.

The Gothic Cathedral is unscathed in the background.
On the stone banks, a couple sits with their arms around each other.
The caption: *Lucky to be alive.*

***

In Al Anbar Province, he told me a boy blew himself up while burying a
bomb roadside. Later, a dog carried away his liver.

***

Perhaps he sent me the photo of his kill because I don't agree with the war.
He wanted to know if I could love him anyway.

***

In the taxi to the *Bahnhopf,* the Beatles song "Yesterday" played
and I thought: *I'm riding to a train station with my high school boyfriend.*
Twelve years apart tried all its tricks against us.
After not touching all morning, he rested his forearm on my thigh.
Willows lined the street, whipped by, and through their bare branches
a church spire. Were it spring, I would not have seen it.

Döner Kebab

I can still taste the hot lamb fat on my tongue.
We ate *schwarma* on lavash, leaning
against the stoop of an Anglican Church.
I asked what he was thinking.
He had retreated into himself more
and more. He said, When we'd patrol
the markets, they'd have these cones
of meat turning on spits in the open air.
Sometimes out in the field I'd dream
of *hajjis* roasting vertically. They'd turn.
He didn't know why
they'd just keep turning like that.

In the Bernese Oberland

When we came down from the north face
of the Young Virgin, engaged, he arranged
for us to raft the mighty Lutschine. At the shack,
they assigned us still-damp neoprene suits,
swim shoes floating like koi in buckets.
Our life vests hung from hooks.
On my helmet, YOU was written
across the forehead, BOSS on his.
In the Swiss air, we began to crystalize.

Stepping in the raft while the river raged
ice-and-mountain-muddy beneath us
was not easy. Nothing about this
seemed like a good time, but he
was already at the head of the raft.
I mimicked the young American girls in our group,
dug in and held on. Once we shoved off,
we had to ride it to the river's foot,
skimming over slick boulders and rock bed.

When the land plateaued, he dove in
the cold turquoise of Brienz.
The girls were wild with giggles,
chattering like sleek lake dolphins.
He beckoned but I did not follow. I was afraid.
I needed him to accept me as I was,
to offer his hand as I stepped out of the boat,
to walk me down the cold and impossible mountain.

At the Farmer's Market in Columbus, Georgia

He sauntered through the stalls,
stopping to palm fruit he didn't intend to purchase.
I fingered the quilts, the wool baby bibs.
I wanted him to notice them. A whirl of fall leaves
trailed behind us. A girl in pigtails
sold corn from a rusty tailgate,
an infant squirrel pouched in her shirt pocket.
It wasn't for sale, but he bought it, promising
to take good care. He put it in the net of his pocket
with the change, and walked on,
musing on whatever else there was to buy.

The Promise

In the letter I read without permission, he wrote, he wished he could marry her instead of me. We weren't right. He still dreamed of her tits in his mouth, her long blond hair tangled in his fists. He told me if I married him he'd never write to her again. He'd never think of her again. He said, if I married him, he'd work every day to make it up to me. He said he'd be more present. He said we'd be happy. I said I forgave him.

Fall Wedding in Georgia

We made it to the Columbus court house
just before it closed. In the disheveled
judge's office, the furniture was common,

metal filing cabinets adorned with fake ivy,
grocery store tile under our feet, and a wall
of windows faced the autumnal south.

The sky was green as pond algae.
Sporadic lightning pierced downcountry.
Leaves swirled up, vortexes.

On a boxy TV, the Weather Channel
flickered warnings of tornadoes skirting
my new trapezoidal county.

We said our vows without meeting eyes.
The elevator down was quiet. We ran
to the truck under the sting of cold fast rain.

That night, we had a reservation
at a mansion turned bistro.
The sky hid its diamonds.

At dinner, we told no one
we were newlyweds.

First Morning

"Ruthless means a promise is nothing."
       –Sharon Doubiago, "Kerouac and Monroe on Kalaloch"

On our wedding night, we fell asleep early
under separate twin quilts,
having spent all our money
on the king-size pillow top
which, lacking the proper frame,
rested on a rough wood rail.
He scoffed at my offer to sew
the mismatched and fraying quilt ends
together. The next morning,
he left to retrieve his daughter
from her mother. I woke motion-sick,
our baby, big as an eggplant,
barrel-rolling inside me. The house
did not smell like pain perdu.
All of it was already
contrary to what was promised.

Housework

Laundry was my husband's
specialty: segregated whites and darks,
the machine's constant churn
like a stomach. He knew the proper way
to fold girls' panties, bras,
lined shirt cuffs to seams, pant legs
to zippers. Crisp, ironed, fatigued,
we always smelled like the mountains.

PTSD

Here in rural Georgia, in the next field over, the Army tests explosives,
the walls of our rental stutter, windows rattle in their frames.

At nine, my stepdaughter's hair is falling out; I find balls of blonde
wisps stuffed in drawers. She looks at her infant sister with disdain.

Mid-night, she comes to our room. Always awake, I see her skeletoned
in the doorjamb, ghost-frail, her eyes dark and glazed over,

listening to the rumbling her father makes. Then she lets a howl go
from her gut, a pack of dogs after prey. He wakes in war,

hands fumbling for his rifle, night vision,
feeling his body for armor, his helmet, his pillow.

Memorial Day

He left me with a hundred unpacked boxes
too heavy to lift up the rented stairs,
the baby, fussy with yeast, just beginning
to teethe, her first ear infection
coming on. The only calls the bill collectors',
only bills in the mail and shiny magazines
filled with pottery I wanted but couldn't buy.
I wouldn't eat for two days so my dogs could.

This was after the fifth kicked garbage can,
the kitchen a mess hall of spilled beans
and coffee grounds, after the hard right
to the ear, the rug burn, the bitten fingers,
after the crushed turtle under his boot.
I wanted to go back to Mississippi,
but I had too many dogs, cats, a newborn.
He threatened to kill whomever I left behind.

A year later, a reporter from *The Citizen*
will interview him. A reward for his purple heart,
he'll get a hero's *hip, hip, hooray!*
down at Schooner Wharf, the old bait
and tackle where he'll gas up his new outboard.
He'll wear a camouflage cap and his Ford
will sport ribbons and bands of honor.

Civil

For our daughter's sake, I'll remember sweat
like an hour glass on the back of his shirt
as he axed the felled branches for winter,
how stove-warm the Georgia house could be.
While I was pregnant, he sometimes rubbed my feet.

II.

"I lost two cities, lovely ones. And, vaster,
some realms I owned, two rivers, a continent.
I miss them, but it wasn't a disaster."
   –Elizabeth Bishop, "The Art of Losing"

The Evolution

"Telepathy is theoretically the next stage in the evolution of language."
    –Henry Drummond, *The Lowell Lectures on the Ascent of Man* (1894)

I.

After WWI, telepathy was all the rage in Britain. One would leave the parlour, while an action or object was decided upon. The guesser would return, mind open. His crown touched another's, until he would dance a jig, or say, *peach fuzz!* Others used it to communicate with the dead.

II.

Imagine a silver tube
                connects your mind to mine.
Now imagine an apple,
                red, without bruises.
Believe that telepathy is real.
                Charge the core with energy.
This cannot be faked.
                I should not try too hard
to sense what you are thinking.
                This will sabotage it.
Keep the transmission short.
                Have patience.
Stay away from skeptics.
                Believe it is real.

III.

There is a tree between two people.

It wilts or grows, measuring emotion.
We suffer when leaves scatter.
Ours a willow, its tongues wag mute.

IV.

It is common, in the aboriginal culture,
to predict the future in the body.

An itch in the right eye: the meeting of old friends

in the left eye: a disappointment

In the groin: a reconciliation

A twitch in the left foot: your journey will result in loss.

V.

Vision in Boston

Above you, a biplane circles,
pulling a banner through
the prism of sun and ice,
the red words I always wanted
you to say, *Marry me,*
or *Live with me,*
                    and mean it.

VI.

Some red string pinned long ago
fastened me to you.
It pulls taut, but will not snap.

The Minor Territories

From any train in Germany,
where my not-yet husband was stationed
after the war, on both sides of the track
I loved the miniature gardens,
their toy sheds spilling a warm glow
onto peonies and cabbage, blackberry vines.
Fortressed by rickety bamboo fences
meant to divide the old ways from new.

Ten years ago, in Baltimore with you,
who'd bring me lilacs for no reason,
I knew this German kind of joy
in a park flush with daffodil lion heads.
After such an arduous winter,
it felt good to go barefoot,
to plant our feet in the wet new grass,
and pass a Frisbee between us.

Now I know they're *Schrebergartens,*
plots of land let by the government.
Almost every city or village has one.
And now even if one builds a shack
they will not let them sleep there. Less romantic,
but think of all those people
studying the fickle clouds, gauging rain,
for whom the past is never past.

Demonstrations

Weeks before the new world began,
we met at an ice-breaker.

I wore coral. The towers still stood.
No one had to scan the skyline for planes.

During the Iraq invasion's first days,
under the sprinkling of blossoms,

I followed you to the capitol.
We held hands through the alphabet streets,

shared a cherry soda, a bag of roasted nuts,
joined a sea of shining bodies.

The anarchists, with their Mohawks and tear-inked eyes,
charged, pushing us forward— one nation then,

rubber bullets whizzing past.
Ahead, the white smoke of tear gas.

I hid my face in your coat.
You covered your mouth with my hair.

I wish our fists in the air back then
had meant more to anyone, even to us.

You wouldn't have gone further north.
I wouldn't have slunk back home

to marry a local boy who liked the feeling
of his fingers on my throat.

Back When Goodnight Took Hours

wet necks and button-fumble
    fogging the windows of your dented Buick
its windshield often an impressionist
                painting under rain.

My hips Matisse-Tahitian   my apartment
a blowze of curtains   open windows
    your palm on my thigh
           under the table
in our graduate class
        on Modern poets.

I had not yet overheard
    your mother say   I was a nice Gentile
         you shouldn't marry.

Our dates were compositions   of shared baklava
warm Italian bakeries   mugs of dandelion tea

    the clatter of almost empty pool halls.

We stole the marbled staircases
        of the Walters Art Museum
glass columns housing
        thin parchments of Rochester
Bibles the Book of Hours.
        Whole afternoons   spent
    memorizing April's Inventory
Heart's Needle   A Locked House.

Late Inventory
After Dorianne Laux

Your hot buttered rye on Sunday face.
Face I kissed, nuzzled, bit with lust,
nose like an L,
          pillow lips,
                    the dark fern hair
along the wooded footpath of your forehead.
Your cheap polenta meal of a face.
Your cherry blossom,
          violin concerto,
                    Madame Butterfly face.
Your flea market face, the friendship bracelet
and afghan blanket of your smile, its loop and knit.
Your red wine teeth,
          hand on my thigh
                    under the table lips.
The free rent, let's move in together of your eyes.
Your rocking chair, iced tea, screened porch face.
Your yellow jacket,
          shirtless,
                    pond-splashed face.
Face that launched a thousand skiffs,
the Chesapeake's lap and pull. Your two-weeks notice
face whipping by
          the window
                    curtained with rain.
Honey and mint, monarch wing and cricket-song
mouth. Maryland summer face.
Your not yet,
          not now,

it's too late face.
Long evening, wait for fireworks, charred hot dog,
picnic blanket face. Lightning bugs sealed in a jar.
Screw the hole-
      punched lid,
            open it up. Set them free.

March Letter, Four Years Late

When I gave birth to my daughter,
you sent a postcard of Gwyneth Paltrow
and her mother, taken by Annie Leibovitz.

In the photo, Blythe Danner spoons her daughter,
hands cinched about the waist she made in her body.
Gwyneth's eyes are downcast in ecstasy.

I thought you'd enjoy this touching
mother-daughter scene, was all you wrote.

My stone-faced husband couldn't understand
why I sobbed for days after, remembering
how much you'd make me laugh:

performing Mr. Roboto in your kitchen
after cooking a dinner of lentils
on your electric hot plate,

teaching me wrestling moves in the empty
living rooms of our graduate school apartments,
your body pinning mine every time.

And how, when I told you I was marrying him,
you warned me not to, because men
after war were never the same.

How they closed up their hearts
in the pine coffins of their bodies.

East Coast Lament

I wake some bright morning remembering
the clean taste of you,

your fingers ribboned in my hair.
My hair less silver then.

Or how you always walked the dark blocks
late back to your sparse apartment.

You used to grab me from behind,
your tongue on my ear.

I left red doors
in dangerous cities unlocked.

Where you went in your mind I wanted to follow,
those narrow paths carved in deep snow.

Then your breezing-in and your mouth
was light, airy, the kisses platonic, then not at all.

I let the last lease run out, willed what wouldn't fit
in the too-small rented car to the sidewalk.

You stood on the petal-blown street.
I drove south unmapped,

not knowing then
what would have made you follow.

Letter From the Velvet Ditch 2

Oxford, Mississippi

The oak floors are dusty with cat litter.
Sweeping is not my strong suit.
Here, small Sesame Street stickers confetti
the leather couch, the slate coffee table,
and magazines flipped through once.
An overturned Easter basket, a bald doll
in a miniature stroller, the crumpled
first page of *Für Elise* furniture the living
room. Coffee's on. Fans whir, ward off,
in vain, the summer heat rising with
the clock. From my desk, I hear the grinds
of the garbage truck at the ready. I forgot
to set out our week's worth of egg shells
and diapers again. My daughter sleeps
quiet. For the moment, she isn't here.
If I close my eyes, I see you, the late
afternoon light on your chimerical body,
what once was the only thing sacred.

Hero and Leander at Market

You called today as I tooled through the Oxford market, and we talked Marlowe and Chapman among the quince and mini bananas. *It's all about delayed gratification,* you said, and I smirked behind the cucumbers. Fingering the artichokes, I said, *Well, you'd know all about that, wouldn't you?* This is flirting for ex-lovers in their early thirties. My daughter swings her legs from the cart, begs for jam. *No seriously,* he said. *Everyone knows it won't end well for them. So Marlowe's using Ovid's trick of putting off. It's really hot.* I remember how my red fingernails on your thigh drove you to shudders. You wanted to wait. We had a year of frenching on street corners, dry humping on other people's sofas. And you were right. The night we finally removed our clothes was like a Coltrane riff, all sax.

Letter From the Velvet Ditch 3
Oxford, Mississippi

I teach my daughter the art of vegetarianism,
      which cheese should be eaten
      with which bread.

How ginger is a cureall for stomach
      and heart pain.

It is good, at each day's beginning and end,
      to quiet the mind, to balance
      the vata.

Chopin's preludes require a light hand
      and a tuned piano.

At night, I read her Blake's *Songs
of Experience*, of Yeats'
      isles in water.

She knows goodnight in French
      and the German of your grandmother.

When she sleeps I clear the fruit,
      from the table
      where we used to play Scrabble.

And sometimes at the sink I'm startled
      by the ghost of your hands on my waist.

Matin

Now, I wake without first thoughts of you.
The dogs huff and whine— first canonical sounds
of the day. Then, what to buy at market,
who to write. Used to, I had all morning
to languish in your imagined arms, your chest
against the pearls of my spine. But after so many
years of not touching, the heft of your hand
on my pyramidal breasts and hips,
your breath's hot bouquet, finally elude me.

Shiksa: שיקסע

To be yours, I would have converted:
Gone the twinkling tree,
the carols and cards.
I would've put away
the glittered pre-school crafts
of my long-dead sister.
I would've refused the ham
at my mother's table,
refused my mother's table.

How disconnected I felt
to the God my family raised me on,
and I wanted to hurt them
for telling me
my small, tidal sister
was not meant to live,
that her death was something *willed*.

I would've changed my name to Ruth,
an alien among your people.
Someone always   *other*.
Back then, you were worth it.
How badly I wanted to listen
to the steady thunder of your heart
every night as we tumbled
together into the unknown
future of our lives.

I knelt before you, made offerings
of rose hip tea and ostrich plumes,
gave the cosmos of your body, my body.

And it was never enough.
In time I've learned
my tongue was not made
to speak your language.

To be Done With Desire: After Seeing you in Boston

"Banishing love isn't a fix."
        –D.A. Powell's "Corydon & Alexis, Redux"

And yet, here we are
mid-thirties with our bellies slumping.
You describe yourself as sickly, withered,
no longer the young college wrestler
who took me out for Indian food
on payday.   And me?

I've grown more robust
with time, my hips spill over,
take more than their share.
Thick swatches of gray cloak my temples.
No more long red fingernails
tapping the bulbs of wine glasses,
no more lilting laughter
late into the night.

After all the years between our former selves
and now,   even now, how you've grown pale,
your reading glasses mark the bridge of your nose,
sweaters hang loose on your shoulders
that have stooped over books in libraries
all these years,   even now I still want

what I wanted then. Maybe even more.
Now that I know
what it is to be without you.

III.

"If we climb our mortal bodies
high with great effort,
we shall find ourselves flying."
        –James Dickey, "Under Buzzards"

When Asked to Say Something Nice About my Ex-Husband

I recall his chest, how sometimes he tolerated
my head on it, strong as a door
skimming the surface of a dark ocean.

First Overnight Visit
Key West, Florida

Before I deliver her to her father's pressed shirt,
I am careful not to notice his ring,
or how his new wife prefers
him clean-shaven, hatless, veneered.
We do not breathe each other in.

He does not ask about allergies, or diapers,
or which is her favorite blue dress.
I drive away fast, tires slipping down Flagler,
past the high school where her father and I hid
from friends. At lunch, we planned our wedding,
debated baby names and nursery themes.

At a stoplight by the Salvation Army,
three men in once-white caps smoke,
string their bicycles with oiled chains,
unaware of the hen with two chicks
humped as rats, pecking near their bare feet.
By example, she teaches her babies

to separate food from rubbish.
They ignore her, scratch their necks,
delight in breeze ruffling feather-fuzz.
Sniff at what smells like a change in wind,
then back to their impressions of children
tumbling after cart-wheeling leaves.

I worry my daughter will love her father
for the swimming and ice cream,
his garden butterflies and iguanas,

that when he returns her she will cling to him,
the way I want to even now.

In Country

My daughter, alive only twenty months,
climbs up to the polished oak table,
to rearrange the tribute of gourds and maize.
She takes a withered husk
in her mouth, new teeth gnaw
the dry texture. Her fingers
grip the technicolor kernels.
Senator-talk moves through the house:
immigration cases on the rise, the need
for protection from outliers.
She flaps her arms like a turkey, feathered
boa slung across her neck.
Her father volunteered to kill
Sunni and Shiite men in war.
I married him for his blue-collar
hands. He liked me tan,
soft-bellied, full with child.
In the desert, he wrote letters
home, the squat script making promises
no one could ever deliver.
But he did, in a way—
this girl who right now is on a mission
to sneak up on the dog,
belly-up in a patch of sun,
clacking her plastic Cinderella slippers
on the tile, announcing herself
to the astral and difficult world.

Letter From the Velvet Ditch 4

Oxford, Mississippi

At the Vernal Equinox, the happy children
scatter like blossoms on the blacktops again,

trying their damnedest to set raw eggs
on their ends. Inside the warm shell,

the viscous albumen protects the sun's
mirror image, riding high. Strange,

working to right what wants to lay
on its side. Any good astronomer knows,

if an egg will sit upright, the earth's axis
has no part in it. What I've learned:

sometimes you have to abandon
a theory when a better one comes along.

Heroine, Cherub-Squat in Diapers

I.

As the September equinox approaches,
my daughter plants her bare feet firmly in clay,
points to the sky, the jasmine, her sandbox,
relishes, *outside,* the one good word she can say.

II.

The dogs are *gods* to be scolded.
She is often wrong. In this small house
we orbit each other, always in motion.
Even in sleep, her eyes flutter, tongue swirls
around a pacifier. Her body contorts
and makes use of the space it is given.

III.

She delights in pudding-smear,
commercial jingles, and long baths.
The shape of my body is famous
to her. I am moon and sun and the light.

IV.

Learning patience, her fingers work a puzzle.
She turns the wooden pieces forwards and aft.
Try as she might, the star will never fit the heart.

Towards Home

When my husband left Georgia,
    he planted his American flag in the sand
of our balmy hometown, began a new family.
    My mother wants me to move home.
I'm fond of joking, *Key West isn't big enough*
    for the both of us. But I envy his wife's freedom
to raise splashing, brown children
    who cheer and play Junior League football
on Friday nights, where every family
    has known each other for centuries, to worship
the sun, to roast a pig on Christmas Eve, to feel
    the wind pick up and call that winter, to listen
to what light says when it changes water,
    to not live in fear of what he will do.

Letter From the Velvet Ditch 5
Oxford, Mississippi

I fired the yard man, thought,
at spring's launch, I'd mow

every other week. Late May,
bull thistle, black medic,

stiltgrass and fleabane abound.
Ragweed grows waist high

against the fence, where nails lessen
their hold on partner boards. I let

the cats roam the neighborhood
after years of keeping them in.

A divorcée, I've learned
to lessen my grip on the world.

Love is in the letting loose.

Coming to Love

My daughter is almost the same age
my baby sister was when she died.

She was thrown, puddled in glass,
they say, lost to us on impact,

but I know she squeezed my hand
as we rode with her in the ambulance

which took too long to find us
at that picnic area between a fast river

and a highway. I am careful
to strap my daughter in her car seat,

but she has taken to wriggling her arms
free of the straps. She does not like

to be hemmed in, and my heart empties
its chambers whenever I find she's done it.

She's grown to look like her forever-
toddler aunt: long shins, chunky thighs,

straight brown hair below her shoulders,
lower jaw like a horseshoe.

As her third birthday approaches,
I think, *What if I lost her, what if she died?*

For years, my mother rocked shut,
wasn't fully there.

She'd circle me with her dimpled arms,
but never long enough, never all in.

When Liv was born, I was drugged.
I didn't love her right away.

Like dating, it takes time to come to love.
I worried her alive, those first months.

Now, I understand restraint from the other side,
the need to hold on tight, then tighter.

Peach Tree, Late Summer

At the nursery, I ask my daughter,
who's two and a half, to choose a sapling.
She trips through the spindly trunks in
black plastic buckets, pulls leaves off
to study them. She even chews them,
spits and wipes her mouth with the back
of her hand. Proclaims, finally, *Apple twee.*

But we're in Mississippi where apples won't grow.
Our love affair with winter is short-lived.
It often blankets our brown river
valley with a dusting of overnight snow,
a delight given then taken back too soon.
Heat muscles in when it shouldn't.

I purchase a peach, because she says
the leaves are shaped like green bananas,
like green half moons, like green sickles,
and because she was born in Georgia
the only place we were ever
a family, though she has no
memory of it, and I envy that.

Digging through clay in mid-September
is like putting a shovel to concrete.
Not young anymore, my knees grind.
The old tennis elbow acts up.
We wet the ground. She holds the garden hose,
and drinks from it though no one's ever
taught her how. I replace the useless
orange clay with store-bought soil.

We plant the tree, old as she is
but twice as tall, and tamp the earth.

She asks if this peach tree will grow apples.
Her first lesson in disappointment.
That what we want is often never
what we can have. Even
second-best takes leverage, sweat,
muscle and bone work. Where we end
doesn't look much different
than where we began. A tree
is still a tree, in the ground or in a pot,
and peach will never taste clean like apple.

Dirge for Morning

All of northern Mississippi is snowed in.
The sun has hidden its face like a child
so long I've nearly forgotten
what it feels like.

Years ago I wanted silence, to work
when the house was full
of sleep–
           cursed the sudden
baby moaning,
an old ghost over the intercom.

I read Snodgrass's *Heart's Needle*
in my ex-husband's leather chair.
Its worn, cat-picked cushions
curve to my curves. Now,
his bloodhound curls next to me,
breath warms my hip, paws
quivering, still icy
from the day's first hunt.

Letter From the Velvet Ditch 6
Oxford, Mississippi

My new yard man is Papa-Don't-Preach-hot.
Today, he came to my garage door

soaked with rain. Cap turned back,
gray scruff on his chin and cheeks.

He was older than I thought he'd be.
His chest and jeans were tight.

Work gloves and billfold bulged
his back pocket. If the weather's good,

he'll be here Monday to turn the beds.
Oh, Monday! I've never looked more forward

to your arrival. Rain– hold off,
so he can get them laid.

Mystery Dad

With lines written by my seven-year-old daughter who hasn't seen her father since she was three

Oh where can he be?
Is he swimming in the canal?
Is he being chased by squirrels?
And what does he look like?
Does he wear jean shorts?
Does he like to fish? Can he
fix a toilet? Does he
say *excuse me* when he burps?
What does his voice sound like?
Is it high and squeaky like a mouse,
or low like a lion? Does he roar,
roar, roar? Can he use the phone?
Does he know how to write
in cursive? I could draw him
but I don't know how.

My Daughter Waits for her Father
Key West, Winter, 2014

When she tries to draw her father,
it's a generic round face atop a stick body.
She does not remember how
his stubble once tickled her cheek,
or being lifted into the air
as if she were no trouble at all.
With small, dimpled hands, she has combed
the hair she just learned to rinse
with strawberry shampoo. Now
under a verdant canopy, she sits
criss-cross applesauce
on the steps of my mother's porch,
dappled by morning light
through the Christmas palms,
sure he will come this time.
Somewhere a dove perch-coos.
A prop plane loops over us,
looking for yesterday's missing boater
among the salt ponds' snarled mangrove roots.
The day grows hot. She wilts
but will not leave the porch.
I stay with her. Some part of me
hoping he never shows up,
not ready to relinquish all
I've been holding onto with swollen fingers.
The white sky is suffocating.
A brown lizard rests on the porch railing.
They have a staring contest until a coconut falls
and spooks him. Perhaps he will come back,
she says, if she builds him a house.

We gather shucked palms and coins of coral.
By afternoon's end it is three-storied
with snail-shell windows and a moat.
The lizard never returns, but we've seen three monarchs
and a praying mantis. When we begin
to slap mosquitoes from our bare ankles,
I tell her it's time to go in. There's cake for dinner.
On her face I see the look of someone told
it's time to give up the search for something lost.
She leaves the work of waiting and turns to lesser things.

My Daughter's Watercolor

At first, her painting is rain-smudge,
a continuous dream of white and black strokes
dripping down the page like Munch's *Scream,*
a wavy apparition with no sound.
A *trompe l'oeil,* she tells me it is
a horror of puppies huddled together.
Their eyes give them away. They look back
at me looking, begging for, *what?*
A question they don't know how to ask.

Nous Sommes in a Texas Parking Lot

When we got back to the car, we split a loaf of French bread between us. The steam lifted from it like a ghost leaving its body. On the radio, the newscaster was saying something about an attack in Paris, a magazine ambushed by gunmen, an unknown number of fatalities. My daughter thinks the word *fatalities* is pretty. It lilts on the tongue like *nightingale*. She wants to know what it means. I want to lie. I want to say, it's a type of bird or a French word for cheese. One day she will know the meaning of all words. She will become afraid of using them without dying.

At Lake Mineral Wells State Park
Mineral Wells, Texas, October, 2015

I have brought a group of teenagers
to study their free country. We hike down
a craggy trail, treacherous with boulders
and wild rose vines, just thorns now
this time of year. The oaks are beginning
to turn. I lose my footing,
fall, but in falling find
a rock with moss shaped like a heart.
Blood blooms through my jeans.
I worry about my daughter. I have left
her at school an hour's drive away.
What will happen to her
if something happens to me? I am all
she has for a thousand miles.
The students and I push ourselves
farther than we think we can go.
Out of dense forest the deep blue lake
opens ahead of us, and we pause.
Leaf shadows vibrate on the humus.
A woodpecker rattles its brain for a taste.
We keep going. My heart limps inside me.
A lizard hurries across my line of sight.
I think of home. The usual pain
of being far from it is lessened here.
Through branches, the sun shows lines
of monofilament. Mid-air, a spider,
small and gray as lint, throws balls
of silk to the wind, hoping they catch
and take hold.

Home

"There was a house, and then no house."
—Mark Strand, "In the Afterlife"

My mother lives now
in the house of her former
boyfriend, across the canal
from the home she owned
for the spell of my childhood.

When I visit, we sit in plastic
chairs on the concrete lanai,
and watch the new owner,
whom we've nicknamed Chiminea
for his desire to burn
anything that will catch a flame
in his fluted clay urn,

swim in what used to be
our pool, soak
his pale body in the gurgling
jacuzzi, where our favorite cat,
Shady Lady, drowned
after suffering a stroke
while taking a long drink.

We try not to glare,
but all I want to do is open
the windows, crawl into
my old squeaky bed, smell
the too-sweet Cuban bananas
my dead father planted

all those years ago.

My mother wants everything:
the tin kitty full of mad money,
my father's garbage truck snore,
both her girls safe, the moon
through the skylight, blessing
our milk-sour mouths slack with sleep.

But they are gone and only
we are here now, and there is no
going back. There is only
now, and now, and now,
and tomorrow, until there isn't.

Acknowledgements

2River View: "March Letter, Four Years Late" and "To be Done with
  Desire: After Seeing You in Boston"
The Boiler Journal: "Late Inventory," "Back When Goodnight Took
  Hours," "In the Bernese Oberland"
cellpoems: "Civil"
Cimarron Review: "At the Farmer's Market"
Consequence: "Letter from the Velvet Ditch 1" originally titled "Thoughts
  From an Army Girlfriend"
Deep South Magazine: "My Daughter Waits for Her Father"
descant: "Letter From the Velvet Ditch 4"
Drunken Boat: "Bad Nauheim Train Station: After War"
[Ex]tinguished & [Ex]tinct: An Anthology of Things That No Longer [Ex]ist,
  (Twelve Winters Press), "Matin"
Gamut Magazine: "Shiksa" and "PTSD" (re-print)
The Guardian, UK: "Heroine, Cherub-Squat in Diapers"
Hopkins Review: "First Overnight Visit"
Iron Horse Literary Review: "Photo of the Euphrates"
Josephine Quarterly: "Late October, Sardis Lake"
North American Review: "A Waiting Room in Kuwait"
Old Red Kimono: "In Country," originally titled "Strange-Countried Men"
PANK: "Demonstrations," "East Coast Lament"
Paper Nautilus: "Shiksa"
Poet Lore: "Memorial Day" and "The Evolution"
Poetry Kanto: "Dirge for Morning"
Poetry Northwest: "At Lake Mineral Wells State Park"
Political Punch: Contemporary Poems on the Politics of Identity (Sundress
  Publications): "PTSD"
Prairie Schooner: "Peach Tree, Late Summer," "Coming to Love"
Proud to Be: Writing by American Warriors Vol. 2: "Beautiful Dreamers"
  originally titled "Talk"

Not Somewhere Else But Here: *A Contemporary Anthology of Women and Place* (Sundress Publications): "Peach Tree, Late Summer" (reprint)

RE:AL: "*Nous Sommes* in a Texas Parking Lot," "The Germany Poems"

Southwest Review: "Fall Wedding in Georgia"

TAB: The Journal of Poetry & Poetics: "Minor Territories"

The Tishman Review: "Home"

About the Author

Danielle Sellers is from Key West, FL. She has an MA from The Writing Seminars at Johns Hopkins University and an MFA from the University of Mississippi where she held the John Grisham Poetry Fellowship. Her poems have appeared in *Prairie Schooner, Subtropics, Smartish Pace, The Cimarron Review, Poet Lore,* and elsewhere. Her first book, *Bone Key Elegies,* was published by Main Street Rag. She teaches Literature and Creative Writing at Trinity Valley School in Fort Worth, Texas.

Other Sundress Titles

Citizens of the Mausoleum
Rodney Gomez
$15

Either Way, You're Done
Stephanie McCarley Dugger
$15

Before Isadore
Shannon Elizabeth Hardwick
$15

Big Thicket Blues
Natalie Giarratano
$15

At Whatever Front
Les Kay
$15

No More Milk
Karen Craigo
$15

Theater of Parts
M. Mack
$15

What Will Keep Us Alive
Kristin LaTour
$14

Stationed Near the Gateway
Margaret Bashaar
$14

Actual Miles
Jim Warner
$15

Hands That Break and Scar
Sarah A. Chavez
$15

They Were Bears
Sarah Marcus
$15

Babbage's Dream
Neil Aitken
$15

Posada: Offerings of Witness and Refuge
Xochitl Julisa Bermejo
$15

Suites for the Modern Dancer
Jill Khoury
$15

Every Love Story is an Apocalypse Story
Donna Vorreyer
$15

Ha Ha Ha Thump
Amorak Huey
$14

major characters in minor films
Kristy Bowen
$14

CPSIA information can be obtained
at www.ICGtesting.com
Printed in the USA
BVHW030610270219
541259BV00002B/25/P